SOME CASE STUDIES OF AIDS PATIENTS IN INDIA

Keyword: AIDS, INDIA

SOME CASE STUDIES OF AIDS PATIENTS IN INDIA

ANKIT P.PATEL

(Clinical Psychology)

SOME CASE STUDIES OF AIDS PATIENTS IN INDIA

Author, Researcher, Illustrator: Ankit Patel
This Special Edition Published, 2015

REDSHINE International Press,
Headquarters(India): 88, Patel Steert, Navamuvada,
Lunawada India-389230
Contact us: +91 9558216314 (only India)

In arrangement with, RED'MAGIC NETWORKS, India

ISBN-13: 978-1-4943-5907-2
ISBN-10: 1494359073

2015 (First Edition)

This special edition exclusively distributed by Impulse marketing.

For sale only in India, Canada, Germany, Bangladesh, Sri Lanka, Philippines, and Malaysia.

www.redshinepub.eu.pn info.redshine@asia.com

Dedicated to,

My Master, Prof. Suresh Makvana

Sardar Patel University,

Vallbh Vidyanagar, India

NOTICE OF RIGHTS:

DISCLAIMER:

Author's Note:

Present work is related with social problems. Presents hypothesis are depends on Psychological method and statistics. So, it can change according to situation.

I tried to control different variable, but some of variable are invisible.

The research is more scientific. Many references are helped me for more scientific results.

ABOUT AUTHOR

Early Biography

Ankit Patel is an Indian Author, Storyteller, Novelist, Critic, Philosopher, Researcher and Counselor. He was born in Navamuvada, (Gujarat-India; 389230) to a middle class Gujarati family. His father is a farmer and his mother a government primary teacher. In 2011, BIGGpsyche Academy of Psychology named him as Influential as one of the 100 most Psychological Authors in India. He writes as op-ed Articles for English, and Gujarati publications.

Education

Ankit's education was mostly in Lunawada Taluka. He attended the 'Palla Pra Shala' (1995-2002), 'Sreyas Sardar Patel Mathymik High School' (2003-2005), 'S.K. High School' (2006-2007), and then studied at P.T.C. College at Ranchhodpura (2008-2009). He completed graduation from 'Sheth. P. T. Arts & Science College, Godhra (2010-2013). He has graduated in Psychology. He studies now in M.A at SARDAR PATEL University, V. V. Nagar, India.

Research Work

*Ankit Patel is a researcher (Since 2009) of the best likes researches of Psychology.

Certificated Researches:

On National Conferences:

- *"A Study about Educational Achievement of Secondary School Student"*
  (Certificate by: UGC Sponsored National Seminar on 'Parenting, Adolescence and Academic Achievement'; Organized by: Department of Psychology, Smt.M.M.Shah Mahila Arts College, Kadi-India, March 2nd & 3rd 2011)
- *"A Study Related to the Co-Ordination Students Under the Grading and Semester Systems"*
  (Certificate by: Council for Teacher Education, Gujarat Organizes National Seminar on 'Innovation in School Education', 24 July 2011, Organized by: Sarvoday College of Education, Samaldevi, Gujarat-India)
- *"MOTIVATION- An Important Requirement in Child Development"*
  (Certificate by: National Conference on 'Child Development: Multidimensional Approach', Organized by: Post Graduate Diploma in Counseling Psychology, Gujarat University, Ahmedabad, Gujarat-India, January 21-22, 2012)

- *"Some Case Studies of AIDS Patients"*

  (Certificate by: National Level Seminar on 'AIDS-Challenges or Curse of Modern India', Organized by: Dept. of Psychology, Gujarat University- Ahmadabad & Jyotivikas Shiksan Sanshthan-Jodhpur, Rajasthan, March 24-25, 2012

On International Conferences:

- ***"Some Case Studies of AIDS Patients in India"***
  (Certificate by: 6th International Conference on 'Management and Behavioral Science', Organized by: SMBS, Ahmadabad, Gujarat-India, December 1st -2nd 2012)
- ***"Significance of Comparative Study of Young Students Life skills In Gujarat State"***
  (Certificate by: 4th International Conference on 'Life Skills Education'', Organized by: Department of Psychology, University of Mumbai-India)

Published Researches:

*With ISSN number:

- ***"A Study on the Adjustment among People Practicing Love Marriage and Arrange Marriage"***
  (Published by: 'GUJARAT MANOVIGYAN DARSHAN', Journal of Psychology for Learning and Research, Vol. no. 2-3, Issue no. 6-7, Apr.-Sept. Page no. 87-89, ISSN no. 2229-3477)
- ***"A Comparative Study of the Co-Ordination of Students under the Grading and Semester Systems"***
  (Published by: 'A CONTEMPORARY RESEARCH IN INDIA', A Peer-Reviewed Multi-Disciplinary International Journal, Volume-2, Issue-1, March 2012, Page no. 410-413, ISSN no. 2231-2137)
- ***"Significance of Comparative study of Young Students' Life Skills in Gujarat State"***
  (Published by: 'CONTEMPORARY RESEARCH IN INDIA', A Peer-Reviewed Multi-Disciplinary International Journal, Volume-3, Issue-2, June, 2013, page no. 243-247, ISSN no. 2231-2137)

With ISBN number:

- *"Some Case Studies of AIDS Patients"*,
  (Published by: Management Research, Editor: Dr. Sunil Kumar and Prof. Bhavesh Lakhani, Page no. 44-54, ISBN-978-93-81505-48-9)

- *"A Comparative Study of the Factors of Personality traits Among Students of Arts, Commerce and Science of Lunawada College (Gujarat-India)"*,
  (Published by: GRIN PUBLICATION, Document No. v213840, ISBN-978-3-656-42314-0)

- *"Need for Life Skills Education Among Tribal and Non-Tribal Students"*
  (Published by: GRIN PUBLICATION, Document No. V229913, ISBN-978-3-656-45749-7)

- *"A STUDY ON THE ADJUSTMENT AMONG PEOPLE PRACTICING LOVE MARRIAGE AND ARRANGE MARRIAGE"*
  (Published by: LULU Publication.Inc, ID No: 13986706, ISBN-978-1-304-24242-6)

- *"SIGNIFICANCE OF COMPARATIVE STUDY OF YOUNG STUDENTS' LIFE SKILLS IN GUJARAT STATE"*,
  (Published by LULU Publication.Inc, ID No: 14003911, ISBN-978-1-304-27163-1)

- *"A COMPARATIVE STUDY OF THE FACTORS OF PERSONALITY AMONG STUDENTS OF ARTS, COMMERCE AND SCIENCE OF LUNAWADA COLLEGE (GUJARAT-INDIA)"*,
  (Published by LULU Publication.Inc, ID No: 14003910, ISBN-978-1-304-27162-4)

- *'MOTIVATION' an important requirement in child development*,
  (Published by LULU Publication.Inc, ID No: 14003900, ISBN-978-1-304-27159-4)

- *"NEED FOR LIFE SKILLS EDUCATION AMONG TRIBAL AND NON TRIBAL STUDENTS"*,
  (Published by LULU Publication.Inc, ID No: 13993984, ISBN-978-1-304-25678-2)

- *"FOUNDATION OF OCCUPATIONAL THERAPY OF MENTAL HEALTH"*,
  (Published by LULU Publication.Inc, ID No: 13993974, ISBN-978-1-304-25676-8)
- *"A COMPARATIVE STUDY OF THE CO ORDINATION STUDENTS UNDER THE GRADING AND SEMESTER SYSTEMS"*,
  (Published by LULU Publication.Inc, ID No: 13993961, ISBN-978-1-304-25675-1)
- *"SOME CASE STUDES OF AIDS PATIENTS IN INDIA"*,
  (Published by LULU Publication.Inc, ID No: 13990423, ISBN-978-1-304-24836-7)

....

*National and International Journals.
**International Publications.

Book Work

Ankit Patel is also an author of best likes Guajarati books.

- *"MINDPOWER"*
  (Published by: SHABDLOK PUBLICATION, ISBN-978-93-81357-36-1)
- *"A Comparative Study of the Factors of Personality traits Among Students of Arts, Commerce and Science of Lunawada College (Gujarat-India)"*
  (Published by: GRIN PUBLICATION, ISBN-978-3-656-42354-6)
- *"Need for Life Skills Education Among Tribal and Non-Tribal Students"*
  (Published by: GRIN PUBLICATION, ISBN-978-3-656-45764-0)

- *"SOME CASE STUDES OF AIDS PATIENTS IN INDIA"*
  (Published by: LULU International Press, ISBN-978-1-304-24839-8)

- *"RESEARCH GIUDE"*
  (Published by: RED'SHINE Publication ISBN-978-81-921346-9-7)

- *"LOVE FOREVER"*
  (Published by: SHABDLOK PUBLICATION, ISBN-978-93-81110-56-0)

In my opinion, Ankit is truly a rising star in the field of Psychology, Publications and miraculously he has done it at such a young age. The whole society and in fact the country looks at him with great hope. My blessings are with him forever…

Prof. (Dr.) D. S. Gour
(Poet & Critic)
G-5, Anandnagar Soc, B/h Science College. (Guj. Ind)

INDEX

INTRODUCTION	15
AREA OF AIDS	27
REVIEW OF LITERATURE	28
OBJECTIVES	30
RESEARCH DESIGN	31
RESULT AND DISCUSSION	32
TABLES OF GENDER DIFFERENCE	38
SIGNIFICANCE OF RESEARCH	41
2012 UN REPORT (INDIA)	44
REFERENCE	46

INTRODUCTION

The present study deals with the mental health of Aids patients. Therefore it is essential that we should have some clear ideas about the scientific nature of aids and mental health. **Human immunodeficiency virus infection / acquired immunodeficiency syndrome (HIV/AIDS)** is a disease of the human immune system caused by infection with human immunodeficiency virus (HIV). During the initial infection, a person may experience a brief period of influenza-like illness. This is typically followed by a prolonged period without symptoms. As the illness progresses, it interferes more and more with the immune system, making the person much more likely to get infections, including opportunistic infections and tumors that do not usually affect people who have working immune systems. HIV is transmitted primarily via unprotected sexual intercourse (including anal and even oral sex), contaminated blood transfusions, hypodermic needles, and from mother to child during pregnancy, delivery, or breastfeeding. Some bodily fluids, such as saliva and tears, do not transmit HIV. Prevention of HIV infection, primarily through safe sex and needle-exchange programs, is a key strategy to control the spread of the disease. There is no cure or vaccine; however, antiretroviral treatment can slow the course of the disease and may lead to a near-normal life expectancy. While antiretroviral treatment reduces the risk of death and complications from the disease, these medications are expensive and may be associated with side effects.

Acute infection:

The initial period following the contraction of HIV is called acute HIV, primary HIV or acute retroviral syndrome. Many individuals develop an influenza-like illness or a mononucleosis-like illness 2–4 weeks post exposure while others have no significant symptoms. Symptoms occur in 40–90% of cases and most commonly include fever, large tender lymph nodes, throat inflammation, a rash, headache, and/or sores of the mouth and genitals. The rash, which occurs in 20–50% of cases, presents itself on the trunk and is maculopapular, classically. Some people also develop opportunistic infections at this stage. Gastrointestinal symptoms such as nausea, vomiting or diarrhea may occur, as may neurological symptoms of peripheral neuropathy or Guillain-Barre syndrome. The duration of the symptoms varies, but is usually one or two weeks.

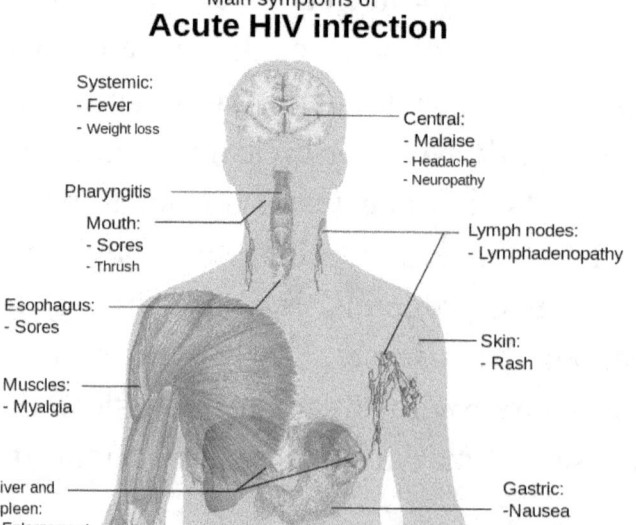

Main symptoms of
Acute HIV infection

Systemic:
- Fever
- Weight loss

Central:
- Malaise
- Headache
- Neuropathy

Pharyngitis

Mouth:
- Sores
- Thrush

Lymph nodes:
- Lymphadenopathy

Esophagus:
- Sores

Skin:
- Rash

Muscles:
- Myalgia

Liver and spleen:
- Enlargement

Gastric:
-Nausea
-Vomiting

Due to their nonspecific character, these symptoms are not often recognized as signs of HIV infection. Even cases that do get seen by a family doctor or a hospital are often misdiagnosed as one of the many common infectious diseases with overlapping symptoms. Thus, it is recommended that HIV be considered in patients presenting an unexplained fever who may have risk factors for the infection.

Virology:

HIV is the cause of the spectrum of disease known as HIV/AIDS. HIV is a retrovirus that primarily infects components of the human immune system such as $CD4^+$ T cells, macrophages and dendrite cells. It directly and indirectly destroys $CD4^+$ T cells.

HIV is a member of the genus *Lent virus*, part of the family *Retroviridae*. Lent viruses share many morphological and biological characteristics. Many species of mammals are infected by lent viruses, which are characteristically responsible for long-duration illnesses with a long incubation period. Lent viruses are transmitted as single-stranded, positive-sense, enveloped RNA viruses. Upon entry into the target cell, the viral RNA genome is converted (reverse transcribed) into double-stranded DNA by a virally encoded reverse transcriptase that is transported along with the viral genome in the virus particle. The resulting viral DNA is then imported into the cell nucleus and integrated into the cellular DNA by a virally encoded integrates and host co-factors. Once integrated, the virus may become latent, allowing the virus and its host cell to avoid detection by the immune system. Alternatively, the virus may be transcribed, producing new RNA genomes and viral proteins that are packaged and released from the cell as new virus particles that begin the replication cycle anew.

Two types of HIV have been characterized: HIV-1 and HIV-2. HIV-1 is the virus that was originally discovered (and initially referred to also as LAV or HTLV-III). It is more virulent, more infective, and is the cause of the majority of HIV infections globally. The lower infectivity of HIV-2 as compared with HIV-1 implies that fewer people exposed to HIV-2 will be infected per exposure. Because of its relatively poor capacity for transmission, HIV-2 is largely confined to West Africa

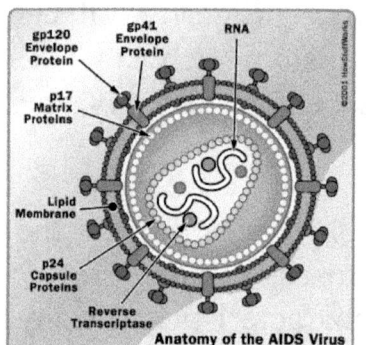

(*AIDS virus*)

HIV stands for *human immune deficiency virus*. This is the virus that causes AIDS. HIV is different from other viruses, because it attacks the immune system. The immune system givens our bodies the ability to fight infections HIV finds and destroys a type of white blood cell (T cell OR CD4 cell), that the immune system must have to fight disease.

(*Effect of HIV*)

AIDS is the final stage of HIV infection. It takes years for a person infected with HIV even without treatment to reach the stage of AIDS. Having AIDS means that the virus has infected and weakened immune system of the patient who body has a difficult time fighting infection, When someone has one or more of these infections and a loss number of T cell, he or she has aids.

If somebody has been at risk of contracting HIV, testing is the only way to find out whether or not he has been infected. The test should be combined with comprehensive counseling by a doctor. The test always makes sense. The person in question is not infected al all HIV is negative. The negative test result indicates absence of infection withed a high degree of creativity. Any uncertainty and any unnecessary fears about aids can be cleared through test, giving negative HIV. On the other hand that someone is infected has HIV positive. This person as a rule will do everything possible not to spread decease further. No one would like to infect his/her

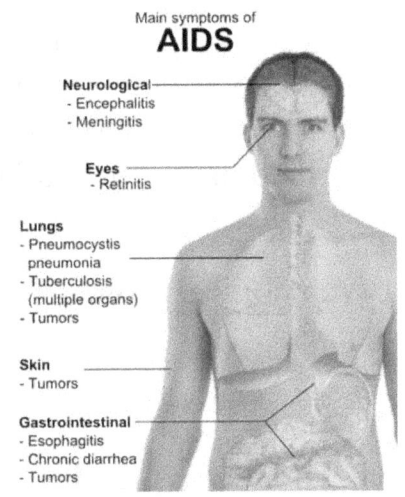

partner. An HIV positive person who himself under treatment can live longer and better, than someone who delays until onset of Aids. It is therefore essential for a doctor to know whether his patients are HIV positive or not. Only then he can make a correct diagnosis and initiate effective therapy.

HIV is infected and transmitted into the body of partner with whom sexual intercourse is carried out.

He has positive HIV virus, he transmit this infections virus if he carries out sexual intercourse with a partner who is totally free from HIV positive virus.

Thus AIDS is a serious, dangerous and infectious decease. It is transmitted through the partner suffering from AIDS. That means it is necessary to safeguard the sexual relations with a person having HIV positive virus or AIDS. Blood of AIDS infected person can become the cause of AIDS being transmitted in to the body of others.

The patients of AIDS are severely mentally disturbed. When the patient is diagnosed as HIV positive he would become nervous and lose his/her mental health to a certain extent. The patients of AIDS are emotionally disturbed, insecure and instable.

The present research is an attempt to find out the Psychological conditions and mental health of AIDS patients.

AIDS in India:

According to a recent study in the British Medical Journal, India has an HIV/AIDS population of approximately 1.4-1.6 million people. According to the United Nations 2011 AIDS report, there has been a 50% decline in the number of new HIV infections in the last 10 years in India. "According to the data released by National AIDS Control Organization NACO, India has demonstrated an overall reduction of 57 percent in estimated annual new Human immunodeficiency virus

(HIV) infections (among adult population) from 0.274 million in 2000 to 0.116 million in 2011, and the estimated number of people living with HIV was 2.08 million in 2011.

The prevalence estimates reported above are suspect. NACO's sentinel survey data indicates over 5.7 million HIV cases in 2001. In 1987 New Delhi announced a National AIDS control Program but that organization spent a substantial amount of time arguing that the AIDS problem in India was overstated.

Despite being home to the world's third-largest population suffering from HIV/AIDS (with South Africa and Nigeria having more), the AIDS prevalence rate in India is lower than in many other countries. In 2007, India's AIDS prevalence rate stood at approximately 0.30%—the 89th highest in the world. The spread of HIV in India is primarily restricted to the southern and north-eastern regions of the country and India has also been praised for its extensive anti-AIDS campaign. The US$2.5 billion National AIDS Control Plan III was set up by India in 2007 and received support from UNAIDS The main factors which have contributed to India's large HIV-infected population are extensive labor migration and low literacy levels in certain rural areas resulting in lack of awareness and gender disparity. The Government of India has also raised concerns about the role of intravenous drug use and prostitution in spreading AIDS, especially in north-east India and certain urban pockets. A recent study published in the British medical journal "The Lancet" in (2006) reported an approximately 30% decline in HIV infections among young women aged 15 to 24 years attending prenatal clinics in selected southern states of India from 2000 to 2004 where the epidemic is thought to be concentrated. The authors cautiously attribute observed declines to increased condom use by men who visit commercial sex workers and cite several pieces of corroborating evidence. Some efforts have been made to tailor educational literature to those with low literacy levels, mainly through local libraries as this is the most readily accessible locus of information for interested parties. Increased awareness regarding the disease and citizen's related rights is in line with the Universal Declaration on Human Rights.

The estimated adult HIV prevalence was 0.32% in 2008 and 0.31% in 2009. The states with high HIV prevalence rates include Manipur (1.40%), Andhra Pradesh (0.90%), Mizoram (0.81%), Nagaland (0.78%), Karnataka (0.63%) and Maharashtra (0.55%).

The adult HIV prevalence in India is declining from estimated level of 0.41% in 2000 through 0.36% in 2006 to 0.31% in 2009. Adult HIV prevalence at a national level has declined notably in many states, but variations still exist across the states. A decreasing trend is also evident in HIV prevalence among the young population of 15–24 years. The estimated number of new annual HIV infections has declined by more than 50% over the past decade.

According to Michel Sidibé, Executive Director of UNAIDS, India's success comes from using an evidence-informed and human rights-based approach that is backed by sustained political leadership and civil society engagement. India must now strive to achieve universal access to HIV prevention, treatment, care and support.

*HIV statistics, 2011 in India					
State	Antenatal clinic HIV prevalence 2007 (%)	STD clinic HIV prevalence 2007 (%)	IDU HIV prevalence 2007 (%)	MSM HIV prevalence 2007 (%)	Female sex worker HIV prevalence 2007 (%)
A & N Islands	0.25	1.33	...	...	...
Andhra pradesh	1.00	17.20	3.71	17.04	9.74
Arunachal Pradesh	0.00	0.00	0.00	...	...
Assam	0.00	0.50	2.41	2.78	0.44
Bihar	0.25	0.40	0.60	0.00	3.40
Chandigarh	0.25	0.42	8.64	3.60	0.40
Chhattisgarh	0.25	3.33	...	...	1.43
D & N Haveli	0.50	...	...	...	...
Daman & Diu	0.13	...	...	...	...
Delhi	0.25	5.20	10.10	11.73	3.15
Goa	0.18	5.60	...	7.93	...
Gujarat	0.25	2.40	...	8.40	6.53
Haryana	0.13	0.00	0.80	5.39	0.91
Himachal Pradesh	0.00	0.00	...	5.39	0.87
Jammu &	0.00	0.20	...	...	...

Kashmir					
Jharkhand	0.00	0.40	...	...	1.09
Karnataka	0.50	8.40	2.00	17.60	5.30
Kerala	0.38	1.60	7.85	0.96	0.87
Lakshadweep	0.00	0.00	...	...	0.00
Madhya Pradesh	0.00	1.72	...	...	0.67
Maharashtra	0.50	11.62	24.40	11.80	17.91
Manipur	0.75	4.08	17.90	16.4	13.07
Meghalya-	0.00	2.21	4.17	...	...
Mizoram	0.75	7.13	7.53	...	7.20
Nagaland	0.60	3.42	1.91	...	8.91
Orissa	0.00	1.60	7.33	7.37	0.80
Pondicherry	0.00	3.22	...	2.00	1.30
Punjab	0.00	1.60	13.79	1.22	0.65
Rajasthan	0.13	2.00	...	...	4.16
Sikkim	0.09	0.00	0.47	...	0.00
Tamil Nadu	0.25	8.00	16.80	6.60	4.68
Tripura	0.25	0.40	0.00	...	...
Uttar Pradesh	0.00	0.48	1.29	0.40	0.78
Uttaranchal	0.00	0.00	...	...	...
West Bengal	0.00	0.80	7.76	5.61	5.92

Some areas report an HIV prevalence rate of zero in antenatal clinics. This does not necessarily mean HIV is absent from the area, as some states report the presence of the virus at STD clinics and amongst injecting drug users. In some states and territories the average antenatal HIV prevalence is based on reports from only a small number of clinics.

History:

In 1986, the first known case of HIV was diagnosed by Dr. Suniti Solmon amongst female sex workers in Chennai. Later that year, sex workers began showing signs of this deadly disease. At that time, foreigners in India were traveling in and out of the country. It is thought that these foreigners were the ones responsible for the first infections. By 1987, about 135 more cases came to light. Among these 14 had already progressed to AIDS. Prevalence in high risk groups reached above 5% by 1990. As per UNDP's 2010 report, India had 2.395 million people living with HIV at the end of 2009, up from 2.27 million in 2008. Adult prevalence also rose from 0.29% in 2008 to 0.31% in 2009.

In 1986, HIV started its epidermis in India, attacking sex workers in Chennai, Tamil Nadu. Setting up HIV screening centers was the first step taken by the government to screen its citizens and the blood bank.

To control the spread of the virus, the Indian government set up the National AIDS Control Programmers in 1987 to co-ordinate national responses such as blood screening and health education.

In 1992, the government set up the National AIDS Control Organization (NACO) to oversee policies and prevention and control programmers' relating to HIV and AIDS and the National AIDS Control Programmers (NACP) for HIV prevention. The State AIDS Control Societies (SACS) was set up in 25 societies and 7 union territories to improving blood safety.

In 1999, the second phase of the National AIDS Control
Programmed (NACP II) was introduced to decrease the
reach of HIV by promoting behavior change. The
prevention of mother-to-child transmission programmed
(PMTCT) and the provision of antiretroviral treatment
were materialized.

In 2007, the third phase of the National AIDS Control
Programmed (NACP III) targeted the high-risk groups,
conducted outreach programmers, amongst others. It also
decentralized the effort to local levels and non-
governmental organizations (NGOs) to provide welfare
services to the affected.

AREA OF AIDS

In the World:

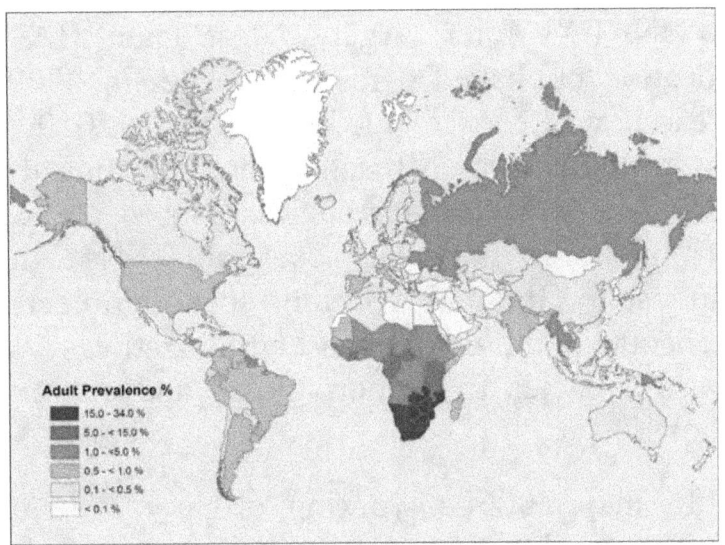

In India:

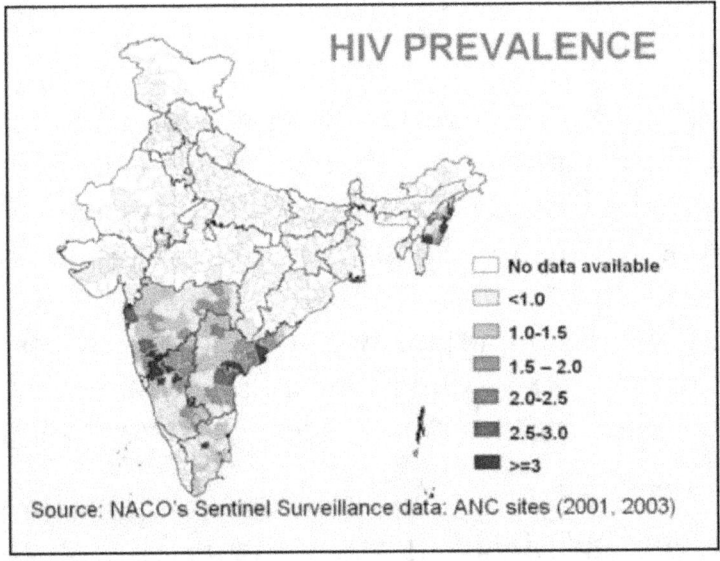

REVIEW OF LITERATURE

A: UNAIDS Inter: Agency test team (IATT) on education published a research paper in 2009. Such research was carried out by IATT for 2010. Global monitoring report on reaching and teaching the most marginalized. The research was carried out with the aim of improving and accelerating the education response to HIV and AIDS. Its specific objectives are to encourage alignment and harmonization within and across agencies to support global and country level actions.

B: In may 2006 a working group of the unaided (IATT) on education was formed to support the main streaming of HIV and AIDS in the G.M.R. IATT administration housed in UNESCO's section of HIV and AIDS in the division for the co-ordination of priorities in education has acted as the agent between IATT and GMR.

C: The team of 2010 GMR on reaching and teaching the most marginal has particular relevance. Children affected by AIDS can face particular challenges in getting educational opportunities ensuring regular school attendance containing their studies. Teachers are given an important responsibility in ensuring that children and young people acquire essential knowledge, skills, and attitudes for HIV prevention.

D: AIDS research alliance help to make HIV/AIDS treatable but 8000people still die of AIDS every day, while millions more with HIV may lose thrill of their lifespan.

As an independent research organization, AIDS research alliance has moved the science forward contributing to the approval of today's HIV/AIDS treatment. AIDS research alliance was the first origination to claim that it is possible to cure HIV/AIDS. Today the world is working to prevent HIV infection. AIDS research alliance is taking steps towards realizing president OBAMA's vision of an "AIDS free generation"

OBJECTIVES

1: Main aim of this study is to know about the patient's emotional stability, adjustment, and self concept regarding their mental health.

2: To know about the patient's present life style.

3: To study and compare the mental health of male patient and female patient.

4: To know the difference between the personality traits of male and female patient.

5: Massage to whole society that all patient of AIDS require more sympathy, co-operation, affection, love, and care.

RESEARCH DESIGN

For present research "MENTAL HEALTH BATTERY OF ARUNKUMAR AND ALPNA SEN GUPTA" was used. From this battery only 70 items were selected for the study, 15 items for emotional stability, 40 for adjustment, and 15 for self-concept. Twenty patients were selected randomly from GODHRA's CIVIL hospital. In this group 10 patients are male and 10 patients are female. When patients came to hospital for treatment, the questionnaire was given to them. All patients answered with full co-operation. Thus data of twenty patients was collected. After that according to MHB the analysis was done. 't' test was used for all case studies.

Variables

In this study patient's illness and present life style are independent variables. Gender of patients is independent variable. Emotional stability, Adjustment, and Self-concept are dependent variables.

Tools

Arun Kumar Singh and Alpana Sen Gupta, 'MHB', National Psychological Corporation, 2005

RESULT AND DISCUSSION

Result of each patient is indication is separate table. Table wise discussion is done below. Final conclusions and significance of research is show at the end. Case study 1 to 10 is male patients and 11 to 20 are female patients.

MALE PATIENTS:

Case study no.1: SHAIKH MAKBUBHAI

Traits	Total Score	Patient Score
Emotional Stability	15	08
Adjustment	40	18
Self-Concept	15	07

*This table indicts that MAKBULBHAI's all score are law in which his adjustment is very poor.

Case study no.2: RATHOR VIKRAMBHAI

Traits	Total Score	Patient Score
Emotional Stability	15	11
Adjustment	40	21
Self-Concept	15	08

*Patient VIKRAMBHAI's score of self-concept is very low. So he is depended on others.

Case study no.3: MAKVANA VIJAYBHAI

Traits	Total Score	Patient Score
Emotional Stability	15	08
Adjustment	40	25
Self-Concept	15	07

*In this table patient's score of emotional stability and self concepts are poor.

Case study no.4: MAKVANA DHARMESHBHAI

Traits	Total Score	Patient Score
Emotional Stability	15	05
Adjustment	40	25
Self-Concept	15	09

*Table no.4 indicates that patient is emotionally disturbed and dependent on others.

Case study no.5: RATHVA SHANABHAI

Traits	Total Score	Patient Score
Emotional Stability	15	07
Adjustment	40	19
Self-Concept	15	07

*These tables clearly mention that patient's mental health is very weak.

Case study no.6: PATELIA RAMESHBHAI

Traits	Total Score	Patient Score
Emotional Stability	15	07
Adjustment	40	18
Self-Concept	15	09

*PATELIA RAMESHBHAI is also disturbed and upset is his life style, which is mentioned in this table.

Case study no.:7 SAMBHALIWALA RAHENADBHAI

Traits	Total Score	Patient Score
Emotional Stability	15	05

Adjustment	40	24
Self-Concept	15	07

*This patient AIDS has affected his emotional balance and his self-concept is also poor.

Case study no.8: GAMIT SANKETBHAI		
Traits	Total Score	Patient Score
Emotional Stability	15	06
Adjustment	40	22
Self-Concept	15	09

*This table is also like another table, that patient is emotionally disturbed and depended.

Case study no.9: TOPIWALA MOHMADBHAI		
Traits	Total Score	Patient Score
Emotional Stability	15	07
Adjustment	40	19
Self-Concept	15	07

TOPIWALA MOHMADBHAI is also emotionally disturbed and depended.

Case study no.10: THAKOR TERSHINGBHAI		
Traits	Total Score	Patient Score
Emotional Stability	15	08
Adjustment	40	18
Self-Concept	15	07

Table no 10 also indicates the same result like another table. This patient is also disturbed in emotionally.

FEMALE PATIENTS:

Case study no.11: MAKVANA JAYESRIBEN		
Traits	Total Score	Patient Score
Emotional Stability	15	08
Adjustment	40	20
Self-Concept	15	05

JAYESRIBEN is emotionally disturbed and her self-concept is poor, which is shown this in table.

Case study no.12: SHEKH RUKHSHARBEN		
Traits	Total Score	Patient Score
Emotional Stability	15	06
Adjustment	40	23
Self-Concept	15	08

*Here in this table patient is very poor in emotional control and more dependent on others.

Case study no.13: RATHVA SUKHIBEN		
Traits	Total Score	Patient Score
Emotional Stability	15	07
Adjustment	40	20
Self-Concept	15	12

*SUKHIBEN's score is different than others, even though she is emotionally disrobed.

Case study no.14: THAKOR AMIBEN		
Traits	Total Score	Patient Score
Emotional Stability	15	07
Adjustment	40	19
Self-Concept	15	06

*Table indicants that AMIBEN is also suffering from bad mental health.

Case study no.15: PATELIA RAMILABEN

Traits	Total Score	Patient Score
Emotional Stability	15	07
Adjustment	40	23
Self-Concept	15	09

*RAMILABEN's emotion and self-concept are very poor.

Case study no.16: MAKVANA INDUBEN

Traits	Total Score	Patient Score
Emotional Stability	15	05
Adjustment	40	18
Self-Concept	15	07

*Patient INDUBEN is also disturbed like other patients.

Case study no.17: TOPIWALA REHAMATBEN

Traits	Total Score	Patient Score
Emotional Stability	15	07
Adjustment	40	19
Self-Concept	15	05

*Patient REHAMATBEN is more dependent on others.

Case study no.18: RATHOR RAZANBEN

Traits	Total Score	Patient Score
Emotional Stability	15	07
Adjustment	40	21
Self-Concept	15	09

*RAZANBEN is suffering from emotional disturbance

and dependency.

Case study no.19: BHIL KAILASHBEN

Traits	Total Score	Patient Score
Emotional Stability	15	06
Adjustment	40	27
Self-Concept	15	06

*This table indicates clearly that patient is mal adjusted with her life style.

Case study no.20: BHIL MANJULABEN

Traits	Total Score	Patient Score
Emotional Stability	15	09
Adjustment	40	17
Self-Concept	15	08

*Here is also the same result, which is indicated in other table.

TABLE OF GENDER DIFFERENCE

Table no.1: Total score of Male and Female AIDS patients. (t value).

Group	Mean	SD	SEM	T	Standard of difference
Male	36.40	2.76	0.87	0.83	1.18
Female	34.90	5.04	1.59	N.S	

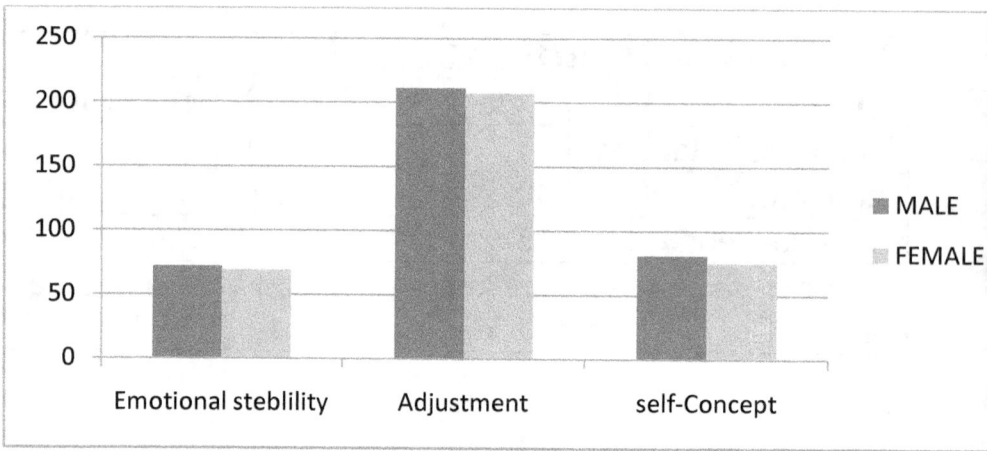

This table indicts that there is no significant difference in mental health of males and females.

Table no.2: Difference of Emotional stability in male and female.

Group	mean	SD	SEM	T	Standard of difference
Male	7.00	1.76	0.56	0.16	0.657
Female	6.90	1.10	1.35	N.S	

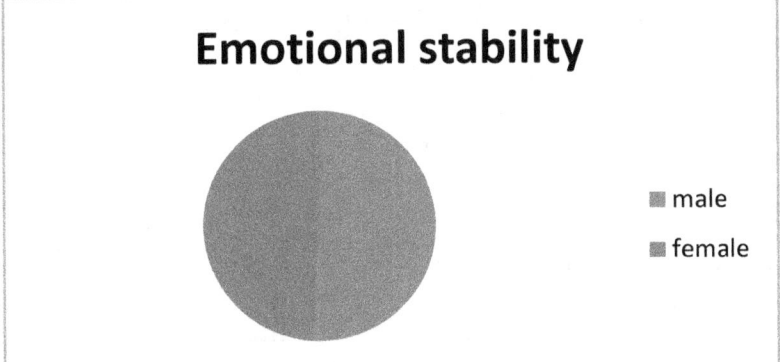

There is no much difference in emotional stability of males and females.

Table no.3: difference of Adjustment in males and females.

Group	mean	SD	SEM	T	Standard of difference
Male	21.60	3.13	0.99	0.66	1.360
Female	20.70	2.95	0.93	N.S	

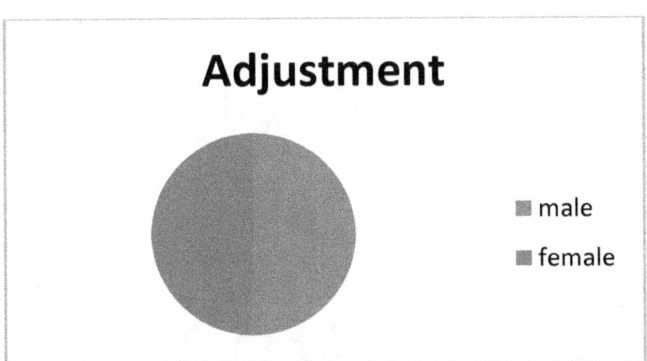

This table of adjustment proves that male and females are equal.

Table no.4: Difference of Self-concept in male and female.

Group	mean	SD	SEM	T	Standard of difference
Male	8.50	1.35	0.43	2.90	0.552
Female	6.90	1.10	0.35	N.S	

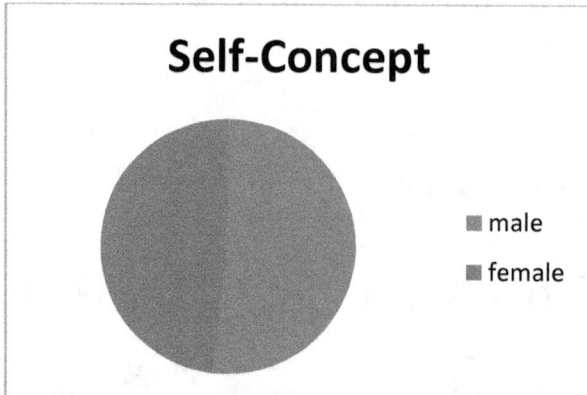

Self-Concept

There is no difference in Self-concept of male and female.

SIGNIFICANCE OF RESEARCH

This study of AIDS patients has proved that all the patients are emotionally disturbed and their self-concept is very weak. Their daily life adjustment is normal. All the patients are under the treatment and they take tablet of ART. At present when this study was done they will live more than two to five years.

Final conclusion of this research is that the all patients' mental health is disturbed due to illness. They are more dependent on others. So they always require help, sympathy, love and care. I request the whole society to behave in good manner with all ADIS patients.

At last if we take care properly and consciously, than we will remove this decease from whole world.

*HIV related infections most frequently encountered in India				
Bacterial	**Viral**	**Fungal**	**Parasitic**	**Other illnesses**
Tuberculosis	Herpes simplex virus infection	Candidacies	Cryptosporidiosis	AIDS dementia complex
Bacterial respiratory infections	Oral hairy leukoplakia	Cryptosporidiosis	Microsporidiosis	Invasive cervical cancer
	Varicella zoster virus disease	Pneumocystis jiroveci pneumonia	Isosporiasis	Non-hodgkin lympho

			ma
Salmonella infection	Cytomegalo virus disease	Penicilliosis	Giardiasisw w stongyloides
	Human papilloma virus infection		Toxoplasmo sis

Rare infections include those due to Bartonella henselae, Rhodococcus equii, atypical mycobacterioses and human herpesvirus (HHS)-8 infections.

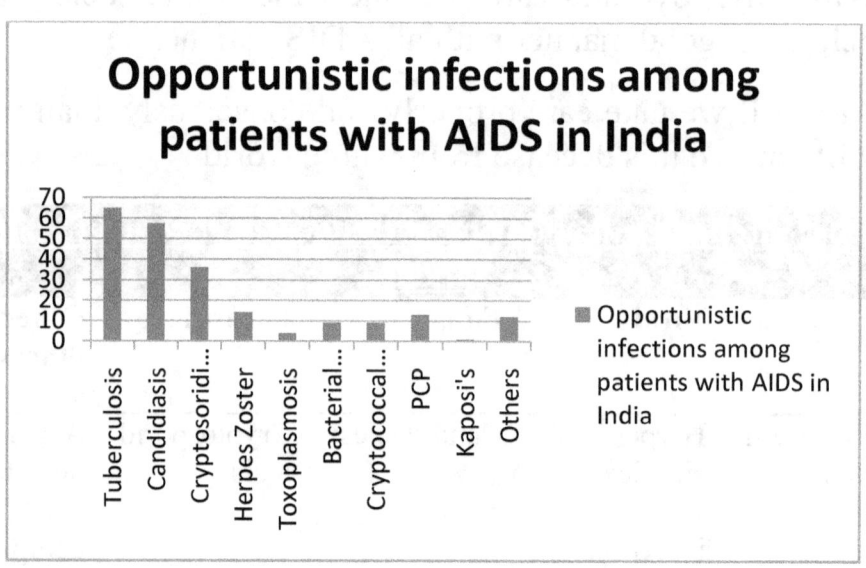

Opportunistic infections among patients with AIDS in India

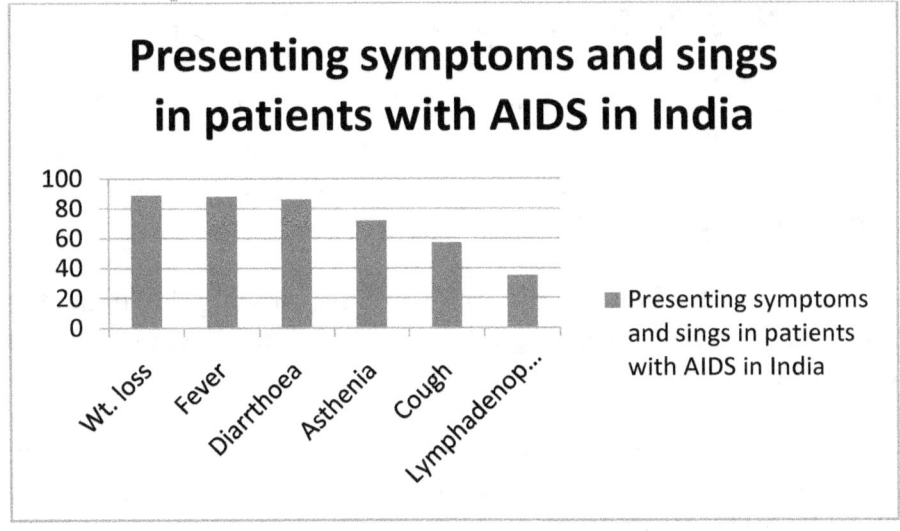

Presenting symptoms and sings in patients with AIDS in India

2012 UN REPORT (INDIA):

New HIV cases among adults have declined by half in India since 2000, according to a new UN report which praised India's contribution to AIDS response through manufacture of generic antiretroviral drugs.

Though rate of HIV transmission in Asia is slowing down, at least 1,000 new infections among adults continue to be reported in the continent every day in 2011.

An estimated 360,000 adults were newly infected with HIV in Asia in 2011, considerably fewer than 440,000 estimated for 2001, a new UNAIDS report has said.

"This reflects slowing HIV incidence in the larger epidemics, with seven countries accounting for more than 90 per cent of people (in Asia) living with HIV - China, India, Indonesia, Malaysia, Myanmar, Thailand and Vietnam," the report 'Together We Will End AIDS' said.

The UNAIDS lauded India for doing "particularly well" in halving the number of adults newly infected between 2000 and 2009 and said some smaller countries in Asia like Afghanistan and Philippines are experiencing increases in the number of people acquiring HIV infection.

It said a total 1.7 million people had died across the world due to AIDS related illness. In India, the figure for such deaths stood at 170,000 in 2009. The report says India has contributed enormously to the AIDS response.

"With 80 per cent of these drugs being generics purchased in India, several billion dollars have been saved over the past five years. The country is also committed to new forms of partnership with low-income countries through innovative support mechanisms and South? South cooperation," the UNAIDS report says.

It also points out that India already provides substantial support to neighboring countries and other Asian countries - in 2011, it allocated USD 430 million to 68 projects in Bhutan across key socio-economic sectors, including health, education and capacity-building. In 2011 at Addis Ababa, the Government of India further committed to accelerating technology transfer between its pharmaceutical sector and African manufacturers.

"We want AIDS free Generation..."

- **BARAK OBAMA** *(President of USA)*

REFERENCE

1: *Arun Kumar Singh and Alpana Sen Gupta, 'MHB', National Psychological Corporation, 2005*

2. *K.Sujatha Rao, 'Guidelines of Prevention and Management of Common Opportunistic Infections/Malignancies among HIV-Infected Adult and Adolescent', NACO, 2007*

3. *Ministry of Health & Family Welfare Government of India, 'ATG for HIV-Infected Adults and Adolescents Including Post-exposure Prophylaxis', NACO, 2007*

4. *K.Jhon,* 'Project of mission is to change the course of this HIV/AIDS pandemic through a unique and comprehensive focus on women', http://www.thewellproject.org, 2012

5. WIKIPEDIA, 'HIV/AIDS', *en.wikipedia.org/wiki/HIV/**AIDS**, 2012*

ACKNOWLEDGMENT

We like thanks to all AIDS positive patients used in this research...

BHIL MANJULABEN

BHIL KAILASHBEN

RATHOR RAZANBEN

TOPIWALA REHAMATBEN

MAKVANA INDUBEN

PATELIA RAMILABEN

THAKOR AMIBEN

RATHVA SUKHIBEN

SHEKH RUKHSHARBEN

MAKVANA JAYESRIBEN

SHAIKH MAKBUBHAI

RATHOR VIKRAMBHAI

MAKVANA VIJAYBHAI

MAKVANA DHARMESHBHAI

RATHVA SHANABHAI

PATELIA RAMESHBHAI

SAMBHALIWALA RAHENADBHAI

GAMIT SANKETBHAI

TOPIWALA MOHMADBHAI

THAKOR TERSHINGBHAI

We pray to God for your good and healthy health…

www.ingramcontent.com/pod-product-compliance
Lightning Source LLC
Chambersburg PA
CBHW070838290526
45795CB00002B/907